To: Eric ?

Sermo

(For A__ ____

Holy Blessings!

Dr. Joseph R. Rogers Sr.

Sermon Outlines For Easy Preaching

Dr. Joseph Roosevelt Rogers, Sr.

2

Introduction

The Preaching of the gospel is a great opportunity to share with the people of God some wonderful and enriching insights that shed a tremendous light unveiling the truths of God. The word 'PREACH' means to lecture, to sermonize, to speak or to deliver the message of the Lord Jesus Christ.

The bible speaks loud, clear and with authority as it relates who must preach and the reason for preaching (teaching). The Apostle Paul writes to the Romans in chapter ten and said, *"[15] And how shall they preach, except they be sent? as it is written, How beautiful are the feet of them that preach the gospel of peace, and bring glad tidings of good things"*!

Why must the gospel be preached? The Apostle Paul writes again to the church a Corinth and said, *"But if our gospel be hid, it is hid to them that are lost."* (2 Corinthians 4:3) So, the Lord Jesus

Christ need lips of clay to deliver His message to the lost, as well as to the believer's for growth, strength and development.

It is my pray that you will find these short outlines helpful as you go into your secret closet (prayer and study time) and seek the Lord's guidance as you prepare for those whom He has commissioned you to share this wonderful, timely and relevant message with.

Whatever you do take preaching serious, in doing so the Lord will richly bless your efforts as you yield your members to the Holy Ghost.

Be Blessed And Preach The Gospel
Joseph R. Rogers, Sr., D. Min

Table Of Contents

<u>"An Unusual Touch"</u>
A Sermon By Dr. Joseph R. Rogers, Sr.
For The Martin Street Baptist Church
Raleigh, North Carolina 27603
Theme: Not Just Any Touch, A Jesus Touch
January 25, 2016

<u>Scripture</u>: "And His (Jesus) disciples saith unto Him, Thou seest the multitude thronging (Large Crowd) Thee, and sayest Thou, "Who TOUCHED ME"? **(St. Mark 5:25-34) (v.31)**

Touch = To feel, contact, lay hands on.
Unusual = extraordinary, abnormal, unfamiliar, uncommon.

Introduction
Our text for the today deals with one of the many **"nameless"** women presented in the scriptures. The "uniqueness of the woman" was that she had a sickness that possibly "ostracized" her form the general population.

We as humans, at least when things are working as they should, possess five (5) senses. These are *sight, hearing,*

__taste, smell__ and of course, *'touch'*. All
of senses are important to our existence
in and under-standing the world around
us.

When we touch something, where it is
physical or mental, we are becoming
intimately involved with that thing.
While I have heard of people losing some
of the senses, I have never heard of a
person losing their sense of touch,
physical or mental.

- ✓ Can you imagine not being able to
  touch things in this world around
  us?
- ✓ Can you imagine not being able to
  touch those we who are dear to
  and love us?

Under the Levitical Law a woman was
not supposed to be touch by her husband
during time of her monthly menstrual
cycle nor was she allowed to come in
contact with the general public.

This 'unnamed woman' in the text
found herself in a somewhat different

situation—she had been bleeding for a long time.

All of us touch thousands of things every day of our lives. Most of them, we do not even think about.

Our touch might be that of love, passion, tenderness, compassion, help, deliverance or that of curiosity. But regardless to the power of our TOUCH, it is never equal to the 'TOUCH' OF THE LORD JESUS CHRIST!

So, our focus to day will be about a **'touch'** that is far **'superior'** to any other human touch—it is about the "Touch of Christ",

In the Primitive Church (Apostolic) some felt that she needed a name this young lady, she is called, "Veronica", who lived at Caesarea Philippi, but no one, knows this for sure.

The reality of this narrative is shares with us a story of this women, who suffered many things at the hands of the many physician, with not positive results. They did not have a solution to fix her situation.

But, Brothers & Sister I am glad to know today/tonight that in spite of man's inabilities to solve life's challenges and problems are "just right" for the Lord.

The Bible teaches me that **"man's extremities"** are God's **"opportunities"**, in order words what man can't do it, God can". You see, while we are trying to figure it out, God is working it out in our favor.

Whatever we need from the Lord, He will come to our rescue, if we mean business. If we have to desire, will, fortitude, commitment and faith; there is nothing too hard for God.

In this text we see a classic example of what can happens when we reach out the Lord—ask seek and knock; The Lord return with a **UNUSUAL HEALING TOUCH**!

Just thinking back a moment, I can remember when the Lord touched me, because it is a **"touch"** that cannot be duplicated by anyone or anything that is on the EARTH. It was a powerful touch, but soothing!

Has The Lord Ever Touched Your Life? If, so are you should continually thank Him for being so a wonderful and awesome God. Now, let us examine His Unusual Touch...

Exposition I

1. <u>The Touch of Jesus is a HEALING TOUCH</u> (It Makes Us Whole)

The Touch of Jesus heals the entirety of humanity-- body, mind, spirit and soul. The healing touch brings wholeness to unwanted deficiencies.

2. <u>The Touch of Jesus is a LIBERATING TOUCH</u>

(It Sets Us Free).

In Mark chapter 7 we can read of the deaf and dumb man. Jesus put his fingers into the man's ears and touched the man's tongue. At that moment he man's ears were opened and his tongue was loosened.

3. The Touch of Jesus is an ILLUMINATING TOUCH
(Brighten, eye opening)

St. Matthew 9:28 says, *"When he had gone indoors, the blind men came to him, and he asked them* **'Do you believe that I am able to do this?' 'Yes, Lord.' they replied"**.

Jesus touched their eyes and said. 'According to your faith will it be done to you;' and his sight was restored".

4. The Touch of Jesus is CLEANSING TOUCH
(Purifying, cleansing)

The story of the ten lepers proves this point. 'Be clean' said Jesus. As they were on their way to the Priest they look and saw themselves 'cleansed'.

Is not it a wonderful thing to know that this day, at this time, in this place--The same can prevail for you and me if we but would only but our trust in the Lord.

Now, as we dig deeper into this text, we find that this lady's situation shares with us some spiritual gems:

1. The Woman's Dilemma:
a. Blood Issue For Twelve Years (12).

b. No results for Conventional Medicine.

c. Condition worsens daily, weekly, monthly, yearly.

2. The Woman's Response:
a. She Heard of Jesus, The Healer

b. She Desired to "TOUCH" Him

c. She had FAITH in Jesus.

d. She Physically TOUCHED Jesus

3. The Ending Results:
a. Her Blood Issue dried up (Immediately).

b. She believed, before she received Healing.

4. What Cause These Result:

a. Her Faith, Press (persistent).
b. The Power of God!

Conclusion

So, we might not have a Physical Blood Issue on this morning, but I assure you that we still might need a "TOUCH" from He who is able to calm the water and still the seas of our lives I want to assure us today that The Lord is able to do exactly what his word says. So, if we're:

- "Sick", we need a touch.
- "Burden", we need a touch.
- "Weak", we need a touch.
- "Lonely", we need a touch...but mostly if we're in...
- "Need salvation", **It Takes Just "One Touch".**

✓ His touch transformed **Moses** the murderer, into Moses the leader of the people of God.

✓ His touch transformed a no body named **Jeremiah**, in the Weeping Prophet of God.

✓ His touch changed **James and John**, the Sons of Thunder, into and Early Martyr and the Apostle of Love, respectively.

✓ Oh! What a "Wonderful" Touch!
✓ Oh! What a "Life Changing" Touch!
✓ Oh! What a "Magnificent" Touch! HIS TOUCH...HIS TOUCH...
✓

- TRANSFORMS THE DISEASED: (St. Matthew 8:15)
- TRANSFORMS THE DEAF: (St. Mark 7:33)
- TRANSFORMS THE DARKENED: (Matt. 9:29; John 9:6)

Whether we are lost, backslidden, burdened, discouraged; we need His touch. Come get it! Just One Touch from the "Master" will change our situations and make everything alright.

One songwriter couched it this way:

"Touch Me Lord Jesus, With Thy hand
of mercy;
     Make each throbbing heartbeat, Feel
Thy power divine.

     Guide Me, Jehovah, Thro this vale of
sorrow;
     I am safe forever, Trusting in Thy
love.

     "Touch Me Lord Jesus, With Thy hand
of mercy;
     Make each throbbing heartbeat, Feel
Thy power divine.

     Now, another songwriter couched it this
way:

     Shackled by a heavy burden, 'Neath a
load of guilt and shame.
     Then the hand of Jesus touched me, And
now I am no longer the same.

     He touched me, Oh He touched me, And oh
the joy that floods my soul!

Something happened and now I know, He touched me and made me whole.

Since I met this Blessed Savior, Since He cleansed and made me whole,
I will never cease to praise Him, I'll shout it while eternity rolls.

He touched me, Oh He touched me, And oh the joy that floods my soul!
Something happened and now I know, He touched me and made me whole.

<u>"An Unusual Touch"</u>
Joseph R. Rogers, Sr., D. Min.
Associate In Ministry

"WHAT MANNER OF MAN IS THIS"?
A Sermon By Dr. Joseph R. Rogers, Sr.
For The Martin Street Baptist Church
Raleigh, North Carolina 27601
Theme: The Only Man
January 26, 2016

Scripture: "⁴¹ And they feared
exceedingly, and said one to another,
'What manner of man is this', that even
the 'wind' and the 'sea' obey him? (St.
Mark 4:36-41)

Introduction

As we find that Jesus continues His
teaching by means of **parables** (stories).
He has taught the parables of the **sower
and the seed, the mustard seed,** but as we
move toward the end of this chapter we
are challenged by the dramatic miracle of
the **"stilling of the storm"**. In this
teaching, we have a striking picture of
the Christian life.

- A life that is never plain
  sailing.

- A life that is rarely has a smooth ride,
- A life that is a roller coaster journey of faith.

- A journey from earth to Heaven.
- A journey of ups and downs.

Sometimes this journey does becomes very stormy and our faith and trust in God is tried or challenged and in this challenging every step of the way.

Not only that but, it appears as though The Lord Jesus Christ is in the hinder part of our challenges **SLEEPING**!

As tumult is going on in our lives, in the reasoning part of our minds, we're tempted to ask-Jesus (Master) do you care? Life's billows are raging, Life's winds are forceful, Life's waves are clapping against us—and we're becoming very fearful of being swallowed up.

- ✓ We feel overwhelmed,
- ✓ We feel besieged,

✓ We feel consumed,
✓ We feel crushed,
✓ We feel beaten,

So, this morning, my brothers and sisters, all of us are going through a storm. The waves of life's sea are hammering our mental and spiritual blocks and we feel as though we're going to be drowned by life's challenges.

Well, that is exactly how the disciples felt in this narrative for morning, even though their 'help' and 'deliverance' is right there on board with them!

The Lord Jesus is tired from the **'stresses'** and **'activities'** of the day and as the ship containing Himself and the Disciples crosses the Sea of Galilee, Jesus lays down and goes to sleep.

As He sleeps, a severe storm overtakes the small craft. The storm is so great that the Disciples are afraid for their lives, but Jesus sleeps through it all.

Then, when they feel that all hope is nearly gone, they wake Jesus up and He steps forth in all the power of His deity and rebukes the storm and calms the stormy sea.

As Jesus demonstrated His mighty power over the elements of life, the Disciples are astounded!

They look around at one another and proclaimed the theme of the message this today, "What manner of man is this?" that even the wind and waves obey His commands. Many of us know about this "Stiller of Storm"-Jesus!

Well, for our spiritual edification this morning there are four (4) simple 'gems or insights' that going to open our eyes—even more as we receive as this great demonstration of Jesus POWER TO HIS DISCIPLES! First...

Exposition I
I. JESUS IS THE STILLER OF STORMS:

St. Mark 4:39-"[39] And he arose, and rebuked the wind, and said unto the sea, Peace, be still. And the wind ceased, and there was a great calm".

A. Regardless Of Their Source:
My brothers and sisters Life's Storms tend to manifest themselves in various ways in our lives. There are storms that are 'satanic in origin', some are 'emotional', some are 'physical' storms, some are 'financial', while others are spiritual.

Yet, regardless to the source of our storm, there is One (Jesus Christ) who is able and willing to stand on the bow of our live and say with resounding authority, "peace be still!" The Lord Jesus Christ is still our stiller of storms, regardless of their source. Next, Jesus is our stiller of storms…

B. Regardless Of Their Force:
Sometimes the storms of life are mild, whereas in some instances the storms of our lives nearly rip our lives apart. But, regardless of the intensity

of life's storms; whether they represent a category five (5) as hurricanes or an F-5 as it relates to tornadoes, we who know the Lord are assured of the fact the God is able to do exceedingly abundantly above all that we can ever think or even ask.

We know two (5) very important things:
1. We will never face a storm alone!
Hebrews 13:5-"[5] Let your conversation be without covetousness; and be content with such things as ye have: for he hath said, I will never leave thee, nor forsake thee".

2. Our God who is greater than anything we will ever face.
Hebrews 13:6-"So that we may boldly say, The Lord is my helper, and I will not fear what man shall do unto me".

Philippians 4:6-7-"[6] Be careful for nothing; but in everything by prayer and supplication with thanksgiving let your requests be made known unto God. [7] And the peace of God, which passeth all understanding, shall keep your hearts and minds through Christ Jesus". Next Jesus is our stiller of life's storms...

C. **Regardless Of Their Course**:
No matter what the outcome of the storm may be, or regardless of what lies in the path of the storm, God will still use it your life for His 'glory' and for your 'good'.

Romans 8:28-"[28] And we know that all things work together for good to them that love God, to them who are the called according to his purpose.

Well, let ask a witness as to whether or not God will bring us out of whatever befalls us in life. Job a righteous and upright man, a man who avoided evil was challenged by Satan; yet in all that he encountered Job, weathered the storm, as he is sheltered in the arms of God.

Even while the winds were raging around him-in the lost of his house, children, livestock and children, Job found the 'grace' to shout praises to the Lord.

Job 1:20-21—"[20] Then Job arose, and rent his mantle, and shaved his head, and fell down upon the ground, and worshipped, [21] And said, Naked came I out of my mother's womb, and naked shall I return thither: the Lord gave, and the Lord hath taken away; blessed be the name of the Lord"

And, I want to encourage all of us to know and received that God can and will do the same for you! I am reminded of the chorus of a song that I heard early in my church experience that goes like this,

"There is no secret, what god can do!
What he's done for others, He'll do for you!
God is Able, God is able, Yes! God is able!
Just to carry you through!
"He Is The Stiller Of Life's Storms"

Exposition II

II. HE IS THE SAVER OF SOULS:
(Hebrews 7:25)

Hebrews 7:25-"*²⁵ Wherefore he is able also to save them to the uttermost that come unto God by him, seeing he ever liveth to make intercession for them.*"

A. He Has Power To Purchase:

My brothers and sisters, according to 1 Corinthians 6:20, "we have been bought with a price!" However, sometime we fully understand the 'glory' of that truth so allow me to share three (3) passages this morning that "unfolds or unwrap" this wonderful narrative as to, "What Manner Of Man Is Jesus Christ" in relation to saving our souls.

1. **Revelation 5:9** -"*And they sung a new song, saying, Thou art worthy to take the book, and to open the seals thereof: for thou wast slain, and hast -redeemed- us to God by thy blood out of every kindred, and tongue, and people, and nation;*"

In this verse, the word redeemed comes from the Greek word **"agarazw".** This word means to "buy in the marketplace." It carries the idea of someone purchasing a slave off the auction block. That is what the Lord did for us when He died and shedded His precious blood at Calvary!

2. <u>Galatians 4:5</u>-"*To -redeem- them that were under the law, that we might receive the adoption of sons.*"

In this verse, the word redeemed comes from the word **"ecagarazw".** This word means "to take off the market." It means to buy something for oneself and the reserve it for your own use. In other words, it is no longer for sale!

3. <u>1 Peter 1:18</u>-"*Forasmuch as ye know that ye were not -redeemed- with corruptible things, as silver and gold, from your vain conversation received by tradition from your fathers;*"

Here, the word redeemed comes from the word <u>"loutron".</u> This word means "to release after the payment of the ransom price." My brothers and sisters, when all of these words are taken together, we begin to get a clearer picture of what the Lord Jesus has done for us in redemption!

B. He Has Power To Purify:

Isaiah 1:18-"[18] Come now, and let us reason together, saith the Lord: though your sins be as scarlet, they shall be as white as snow; though they be red like crimson, they shall be as wool".

Revelations 7:14-" [14] And I said unto him, Sir, thou knowest. And he said to me, These are they which came out of great tribulation, and have washed their robes, and made them white in the blood of the Lamb".

As believers of The Lamb, Jesus Christ, we as saints of God have been washed white in the blood of the Lamb! When we trusted Jesus for salvation, we were washed whiter than snow and every dirty thing we had ever done, or ever will do was washed away from us forever! We have been declared righteous by the

27

Heavenly Father and all of our many sins have been forever washed away.

He Is The Stiller Of Storms!
He Is The Saver Of Souls!

Conclusion

So, as I close this message, it is a wonderful thing to know that we have a stiller of life's storms, and a saver of our souls, but there is one more pieces to this model and that is, Jesus…

IV. **HE IS THE SHEPHERD OF SHEEP**:
Psalms 23-1-"[1] The Lord is my shepherd, I shall not want". How do we know that the Lord is our Shepherd? Well,

A. **He Feeds Us**:
As we make our way through this life we can count on the Lord to give us what we need to help us to grow in Him. The shepherd leads his sheep to the green pastures where they can feed and where they can grow.

The Lord leads us through the green pastures of His Word where our souls can feed on the bounty fed.

B. **He Leads us**:
Not only is the Shepherd responsible for "feeding his sheep", but he must "lead them as well". The Good Shepherd leads His flock in many ways…

- In The Right Path!
- In The Right Peace!
- With The Right Protection!
- With The Right Provisions!
- To The Right Place!

What manner of man is this? There aren't enough adjectives in the collective vocabularies of humanity to adequately describe Him and His glory.

One of the best we can do is to join our voices with that of the **Shumanite woman** in Song Of Solomon 5:16 and declare together that "He is altogether lovely!"

If you need Him this morning,

- He is still the, "stiller of life's storms",
- He is still the, "saver of our souls", and
- His is still the, "shepherd of his sheep".

Why not come to Him and get acquainted with The Man, Jesus Christ who is always riding on the boats of our lives, stilling all storms that challenge us.

And, let us follow the example of **Lawrence Matthews and Inez McLendon** as they sung together the chorus of a song that goes like this: (paraphrased)

> **Just let Jesus fix it for you,**
> **For He knows Just want to do.**
> **Whenever you pray,**
> **Just let Him have His way.**
> **Let Jesus will fix it,**
> **Oh! Jesus will fix it for you!**
> **"What Manner Of Man Is This"**
> Joseph R. Rogers, Sr., D. Min.
> Associate In Ministry

"You Can't Make Me Doubt Him"
A Sermon By Dr. Joseph R. Rogers, Sr.
For The Martin Street Baptist Church
Raleigh, North Carolina 27601
Theme: Remaining In/With The Lord
January 7, 2016

Scripture: "And when they had *sung an hymn*, they went out into the **Mount of Olives**. Peter said unto Him, though I should 'die' with Thee, yet I will not "deny Thee". Likewise, also, "said" all the disciples". **(St. Matthew 26:30, 35)**

Introduction

"One of the most devastating "enemy or foe" in the body of Christ, is "Doubt". Doubt, my brothers and sisters, in many cases, causes a lot of us to lose or miss the blessings that God has in store for us.

Doubt, of which is, **hesitation, uncertainty, suspicion, or skepticism;** and "Fear", of which is, **terror, horror, anxiety or distress,** are **very powerful tools** and they had the ability to will bring the average "**person**" to their

31

knees, if they allow then to take hold and mature in your life (enter mind, then heart).

Usually we as a church family always remembers The Disciple Peter, as being that Apostle of with the **"Big"** mouth, but this text allow us to see that he was **not alone**--all of the other disciple made some vow to Jesus, as to not deny or betray Him.

As Christians we must at all times maintain **'confidence'**, of which is, **self-assurance, sureness, buoyancy, or coolness,** in Our Risen Lord.

The bible teaches in **St. Mark 9:23**- "Jesus said unto him, **"If thou canst believe,** all things are possible to him that believeth".

The scripture also teaches in **Philippians 4:13**—"I (we) can do all things through Christ which strengthen me (us)".

It is within the Words of Christ that our **hope, endurance, survival and**

fortitude lie. Today, my brothers and my sisters, outside of the Word of the Lord you are: **defeated, powerless** and **joyless.**

In retrospect, in/with Christ you and I already have the **"Victory".** All you have to do is to allow the Lord work out things in our life in His own time.

The Old Testament teaches is in **Habakkuk 4:2...**"<u>**but the just live by his faith**</u>". Faith not only means **"believing God",** but allowing that same God to use you in action and application as you **"step out"** upon His Word.

When trouble comes and it appears as though there is no way out of what you are in: remember the one of the great hymns of the church, <u>**"Rock of Ages, Cleft for me, Let me hide myself in Thee".**</u>

Because, we know with **confidence** and **assurance** that:

- When troubled times arises God will **hide us** in His pavilion and

33

in the secret place of His tabernacle.

- When our enemies come upon is to eat up our flesh, they **will stumble** an fall.

- When a host shall encamp around about us and war shall rise against us, we will remain confident.

Yes, we do get tired in **battles, conflicts** and **evil engagements,** but in this **situations and struggle,** we remember second letter of the Apostle Paul to the church at Corinth, stating,

- **We are troubled, yet not distressed,**
- **We are perplexed, yet not despaired,**
- **We are persecuted, yet not forsaken,**
- **We are cast now, yet not destroyed...That is why...**

Exposition I

So, in closing, I can assure all of us here today that we going to have some difficult day every now and then, but through all of them, we must rest confidently in the Lord.

We must practice the action of The Apostle Peter and the other disciples, as they said unto Jesus Christ, though I should 'die' with Thee, yet I will not "deny Thee". Likewise, also "said" all the disciples", and follow through with it.

On this **Christian Journey** we must be aware of the bumps in the roads, **the sharp curves** and **the dangerous valleys and hills**, but thanks, be unto the Lord, this text teaches us to **"Never To Doubt The Lord"**. Never say **I can't do this** or **I can't do that,** but with assurance and confidence always said, **"I CAN"—"I CAN"**! So...

**Never again, <u>confess lack</u>,

"For God shall supply all of you needs according to His riches in glory by Christ Jesus". **(Philippians 4:19)**

**Never again, <u>confess fear</u>,
"God hath not given us the spirit of fear, but of power, and of love and of sound mind ". **(2 Timothy 1:7)**

**Never again, <u>confess sickness</u>,
"For with or by His stripes I am healed (Is.53:5).
"Jesus, Himself took my infirmities and bare my sickness. **(St. Matthew 8:17)**

**Never again, <u>confess worry or frustration</u>,
"For I am casting all my cares upon Him, who careth for me". **(1 Peter 5:7)**

**Never again, <u>confess loneliness</u>,
"For Jesus said, Lo, I am with you always, even unto the end of the world". **(St. Matthew 28:20)**

**Never again, <u>confess weakness</u>,
"The Lord is the strength of my life; of who shall I be afraid"? **(Psalm 27:1b)**

Conclusion
So in closing, we must **maintain, develop** and **apply** the "fortitude" that

God has given us and maintain the "resolve" of the Apostle Peter and the other disciples as they said, "…though we should 'die' with Thee, yet we will not "deny Thee".

The Lord Jesus Christ let them know that they we going to be **offended** that very night, because He, (The Shepherd), shall be smitten and the sheep shall scatter.

Then Peter said, "All may be offended, yet I will never deny Thee". Jesus said unto him, "Before the cock crow, thou shall deny me thrice". But Peter said again, **"I will never deny Thee, as they all."**

But, in the Hall of Judgment, The Disciple Peter forgot about all that he had said, and **Vehemently**, Peter denied Our Lord-three times.

But **At Pentecost**, after the coming of the **Holy Ghost** to indwell the Believers, this **same Disciple Peter** Stood

Up and preach so well that three thousand (3000) souls accept The Lord as Savior!

My brothers and sisters we must not 'forsake' or 'deny' the Lord. Because the bible teaches that if we deny Him before men, He will do us the same way when we stand before the Father. We must hold the Lord **unchanging hands**…

- In the midst of **'trouble'**, don't doubt Him!
- In the midst of **'challenge'**, don't doubt Him!

- In the midst of **'heartache'**, don't doubt Him!
- In the **'heat of the day'**, don't doubt Him!

- When **'storm clouds'** hover over, don't doubt Him!
- When **'violet winds'** are blowing, don't doubt Him!
- When **'choppy waves'** rage tireless, don't doubt Him!

Just sing with **confidence** and
assurance...one of the old hymns of the old
church hymn that goes like this...

- ✓ You can't make me doubt Him!
- ✓ You can't make me doubt Him!
- ✓ I know too much about Him!
- ✓ You can make me doubt Him, in my
  heart!

I feel the fire burning! I feel the
fire burning!
A little wheel a turning! A Little
wheel a turning!

- ✓ You can't make be doubt Him,
- ✓ You can't make me doubt Him,
- ✓ I know too much about Him!
- ✓ You can't make be doubt Him, in
  my heart!

Why? Because, Jesus has just been
too **"GOOD"** TO ME!
I can't speak for you, but **I have a
story**—and you ought to have story!

- When we were **'down'**, Jesus picked
  me up!

- When we were **'weak'**, Jesus made me strong!

- When we were **'sad'**, Jesus gave me joy!

- When we were **'confused'**, Jesus gave me comfort!

- When we were **'burden'**, Jesus gave me consolation!

We should rejoice because of what the Lord **has done, is doing** and **will do** for me in the **future...**
        <u>**You Can't Make Me Doubt Him**</u>"
Joseph R. Rogers, Sr., D. Min.
Associate In Ministry

<u>"Watch Them Church Birds"</u>
A Sermon By Dr. Joseph R. Rogers, Sr.
For The New Beginning Baptist Church
Henderson, North Carolina
Theme: Watch Who Associate With
December 4, 2015

Scripture: "And when He putteth forth His own sheep, He goeth before them and the sheep **follow Him**: for they **-know- His voice**. And **a stranger** will they not follow, but will **flee from him**: for they **-know not-** the **voice of a stranger**". The **Thief (Satan)** cometh not but for **to steal, to kill and to destroy**: **I am** come that they might have **life** and that they might have it **more abundantly**" (**St. John 10:4, 5, 10**)

Introduction

My brothers and sisters it is vital that we understand the importance of **who we associate with**. We are **creatures of habit** and **adaptation,** so therefore who we **run or walk** with, could affect **our behavior** or **actions.**

Therefore, we must follow the bible when it states: **light and dark have no fellowship, God and Bail have no fellowship** and **those who are unequally yoke together have no fellowship.** As a matter of fact the bible says, **"Touch not, Taste not, and Handle not"**—the **unclean things of this world"**.

There are people today that find themselves on the **negative side of the law,** only because they did not watch who they associated with.

There are people today that find themselves with **a deranged marriage,** only because they did not watch who they associated with.

There are people today that find themselves **without the wholesomeness of a loving home,** only because they did not watch who they associated with.

There are church folks today that find themselves **without the richness of the glory of God Word, Power & Anointing,** only because they did not watch who they associated with.

My brothers and sisters, I am concerned about the **atmosphere of the Church**—it should be a **loving enriching experience**, where people can come and get **delivered from** whatever is **lacking in their lives. Delivered** from, **sin, bondage, fears, sickness** and **disease, strongholds** and **schisms.**

Well, today/tonight this day/night it is my prayers that God will **us learn** the importance of watching our associates—and **cling to those thing that have our best interest at heart.**

Exposition I
Well, in this text The Apostle John shared some **important spiritual insights,** as it relates to **our associating with the right crowd.** This text unfolds to us the importance of having a **Good Shepherd** and **following Him/Hers.**

Very simply the text states: "The Lord putteth forth His sheep, **He goeth**

43

before them and the **sheep follow Him;** for **they know His voice"**. But, in contrast they will not follow **stranger,** because they **do not recognize his voice.**

In verse ten, John gives the **contrast** of the **Good Shepherd** and **The Thief.** The **Thief** comes to: **Steal, Kill** and **Destroy.** The **Good Shepherd** comes that we might have **life, abundantly.**

To enlighten us even more the Holy Ghost wants to share some **important information** that will **help us along the way.** We will use **"Birds"** in this lesson:

Birds migrate each year from the **north to the south,** to **escape** the **unpleasant temperatures.** Well, there are **"Birds"** in the church **that migrate also,** because of their **own selfish desires** and **attitudes.**

They are: **Robins, Blue Jays, Ravens, Hawks, Parakeets, Buzzards, Owls, Ostriches, Cockatoos, Road Runners,** and **Peacocks, Doves** and **Eagles**...to name a few. Now, each bird is **distinct** in its behaviors, **looks** and **activities**. Well, so are the **"Church Birds"** in their own way.

It is a fact that **God used birds** in trying to convey unto His people a **message** or to **help them in times of need:**

God use the **"Dove"** during the days of the flood to **help Noah** to **know when the waters had receded** (Gen. 8). The **High Priest** also, used the **"Dove'** during time of sacrifice.

God use the **"Raven"** to feed the Prophet Elijah during the **time of great famine** (no rain for 31/2 years).

So, in spite of the **behaviors** of some birds: **Vaulgers** who are **scavenger** and eat the **succumb of the food change;** there are other birds: like the **"cardinal"** = state bird and the **"eagle"** = national bird who have **different behaviors.**

Exposition II
Now, let us observe these **"Birds"** in their natural arena and **contrast** them to

the **church arena**: Of which, I hope we **do not emulate.**

1. Owl – big eyes and the sight of one will frighten you. The Owl only operates in the darkness of the night because of their keen night vision.

<u>**The Church Owl**</u> = intimates others in the church with their looks and they try to instill fear into them. They operate **undercover, overtly** & **covertly.** Watch them **"Church Owls".** Next there is a…

2. Parakeet – their vocabulary is limit and they cannot say too to many words or complete sentences, but yet they are easy to train and can be taught to repeat word or phrases.

<u>**The Church Parakeet**</u> = Now the Church Parakeet appears to be very humble when they first come into the church family, but as soon as they learn a little, it goes to their heads.

They are smarter in two weeks than some of us who being around for twenty, thirty years or forty years. The Church Parakeet love caring and bring bones among the church fellowship. **Watch them "Church Parakeets"**. Next there is a...

3. Ostrich - they have long necks that can reach great distances. When they **hold their heads down their vision is limited.** Even though they are part of the "Bird Family", they are **not able to fly** as other birds.

The Church Ostrich = The Church Ostrich high minded, because of their selfish attitude and pride; not realizing that, humbleness is **the secret to spiritual elevation.**

Most of the time there **long necks that are stuck in someone else business.** They operate from an 'artillery position"–they are the ground forces! Watch Them **"Church Ostrichs"** Next there is a...

4. Cockatoo - these birds disturbs

the rest of the birds family by making noises over and over again. They just will not be quite. Thy love attention in any form.

The Church Cockatoo = The Church Cockatoo are Always spreading discord in the church and they disrupt the flow of unity of the fellowship. These birds are **agitators** and rumor starters. They are excellent at **getting things** started in the church and the act as those they know nothing.

In church **meetings** and **services**, **The Cockatoo** is always **murmuring**, **grumbling** and complaining about everything that is going on the in church. They complain about:

- **The pastor's** sermon,
- **The choir's** singing,
- **The deacon's** prayer,
- **The usher's** collecting the offering,
- **The announcer's** tone of voice during announcement time, and

yes, even the benediction. Watch Them **"Church Cockatoos"**. Next there is a...

5. Road Runner – swift on their feet, very tricky and hard to catch. They are always confident of their ability to escape the scene.

<u>**The Church Road Runners**</u> – always doing things and its usually **wrong**! Because of the lack of knowledge and crafty behavior they start trouble and get others charge up and they walk away.

They throw rocks and hid their hands. Because of the **swiftness** they are good at doing things and quickly leaving the scene of the crime. Watch Them **"Church Road Runners"** Next there is a...

6. Vaulger – The Church Vaulgers or come on the scene to clean up the kill and eat the scum of leftovers. Inwardly they have a course digestive system to digest all of that filthy intake.

The Church Vaulger/Buzzard = The Church Vaulgers are nothing but human garbage can and likes all of the latest **gossip and hot news.**

They always **run in packs (groups)** and never venture out alone—they have a loud bark, but no guts! They even have the ability to play dead, if necessary! Watch Them **"Church Vaaulgers/Buzzards".** Next there is…

7. The Peacock - beautiful looking, but ugly within. They are **pleasant or pleasing** to the eye. They use their body **to attract you to them** or to **distract you before they go in for the kill.**

The Church Peacock = The Church Peacock looks like the real thing, act like the real thing, but soon change their appearance once they **get where they want to be** (position wise). When that happen the mask comes off, and the true colors are revealed.

The Church Peacocks are all over the church ministries, not for good but the cause all kinds of trouble. With their **changing abilities**, they 'sing' with the choir, 'usher' on the floor, serving only to **get attention to themselves** and **cause division among the church fellowship**. Watch Them **"Church Peacocks"**.

Conclusion

So, in closing I hope that you're not **one or a number of the above mentioned "Church Birds"**.

However, there are a few other **"Church Birds"** that I would like to tell you about that are better '**examples** and **models'** than those that I have describes. They are...

8. The Robin – The Robin is busy gathering food for their young and attending to their own business. Likewise...

A. **The Church Robins** =
**Church Robin studies the Word of God and come to Bible Study.

Church Robin is interested in Church growth and development.

Church Robin is poised to help others and don't mind giving of themselves for the cause.

Church Robin has the qualities of the Good Samaritan, willing to help even in danger. Then there is…

9. The Dove – harmless, caring, pure and they are good example. Likewise

A. The Church Dove =
The Church Dove cares for the welfare of the Church and others.

The Church Dove possesses the fruit of the Spirit.

The Church Dove is filled up with the Holy Ghost and lead by the same.

The Church Dove is easy to get alone with and supports the vision.

Well, I hope that you are one of these **"Birds"**, as it relates to 'character', 'discipleship', 'stewardship' and 'integrity'. But, there is one more **"Bird"** that **The Holy Ghost** would like to describe to us:

10. The Eagle - The Eagle fly high, possesses excellent vision and have great wing strength and span.

A. <u>The Church Eagle</u> =
****The Church Eagle** has the ability for fly either **fly in the storm** or **against the storms** (challenges or situations of life)

****The Church Eagle** stays ahead of the enemy by keeping him in front of him.

****The Church Eagle** warns and protects the flock of apparent approaching problems and situation.

So, my brothers and sisters, which of **"Bird"** are you? I hope you're either the:

a. **Robin** = busy attending your own affairs and helping others.
b. **Dove** = harmless and gentle, sweet and lovable; caring.
c. **Eagle** = insights, knowledge, durability and strength.

Well, you should know that **"Birds"** of a feather **flock together**. It is a fact, that 'A **Tree"** is known by its **fruit**. A person is **known** by the **company they keep. Follow Jesus**!

Let's commit ourselves to follow the lyrics of an old church hymn which goes like this:

"I have decided to follow Jesus; I have decided to follow Jesus; I have decided to follow Jesus; No turning back, no turning back.

Though no one joins me, I still will follow; Though no one joins me, I still will follow; Though no one joins me, I still will follow; No turning back, no turning back.

The world behind me, the cross before me; The world behind me, the cross before me; The world behind me, the cross before me; No turning back, no turning back".

Will you decide now to **follow Jesus**? Will you decide now to follow Jesus? No turning back, no turning back.

"Watch Them Church Birds"

Joseph R. Rogers, Sr., D. Min.
Associate In Ministry

"A Heart For Him"
A Sermon By Dr. Joseph R. Rogers, Sr.
For The Martin Street Baptist Church
Raleigh, North Carolina 27610
Theme: Loving Him Dearly
January 28, 2016

Scripture: "[16] My beloved **is mine**, and I **am his**: he feedeth among the lilies. [17] Until the day break, and the shadows flee away, turn, my **beloved** and be thou like a 'roe' [deer] or a young 'hart' [male] upon the **Mountains of Bether**" {can also be known as **"Bethel"**—the House of the Lord) is the mountains when Jacob, fleeing from the wrath of his brother Esau, falls asleep on a stone and dreams of a ladder stretching between Heaven and Earth and thronged with angels .   **(Song Of Solomon 2:16, 17) (Read 5:1-16)**

Introduction
In reading the Old Testament, **The Song of Solomon** holds a special place in the Word of God. While much of the Bible deals with 'history' and with 'doctrine', the Song of Solomon is a collection of

what is called, **"Love Songs"**. These songs detail the love life of **King Solomon** and **one of his many wives**.

There are many people who do not fill that this writing has a place in the Bible because it is filled with **explicit descriptions of a romantic love between a husband and his wife**.

Yet, if we take a deeper look or observation, we can see a clear picture of the **love relationship between the Lord Jesus Christ and those who are saved by His grace**.

In the passages that are before us, we are given a **glimpse inside the heart of the bride**. We are given the opportunity to see just how **much she loves her husband**. In these verses of this text, we see that she has **"A Heart For Him"**.

I would suggest to you that you take some time and **re-read all of these songs**, that you might get a thorough in depth picture of how wonderful our **Heavenly**

Bridegroom, "The Lord Jesus", is. You will discover **afresh** and **anew understanding** of just **how much we should love Him** and how the degree of His Love for us. Frist, we Observe...

Exposition I

I. <u>**THE BRIDE DOZING**</u>: (5:2-5) (Drowsy, Sleepy, Nodding)

All through the first part of the book, the bridegroom has been referring to this woman as the **"bride"**.

Here, he does not use that term. It may be that they have been **married for a while** when the events that are before us took place.

It may be that the **newness of marriage has worn off their relationship**. After all, when this chapter opens, we find the **bride asleep** and the bridegroom outside her chamber trying to gain access. **Yes! She is dozing!**

We all remember how exciting it was in those first days of our relationships. We all remember the **thrill** of "**the first** love". Will we admit to the fact that we find ourselves in or moving in the direction of this couple—the thrill is diminishing somewhat!

We are so 'secure' and 'satisfied' in what we have that we have forgotten the One (Jesus Christ) who gave us all we have. I am thrill to know that we have a Christ relationship that keeps us on our toes.

A. The 'Call' Of The Beloved: (Bride, Husband) (5:2)
Notice how tender His call is. He uses terms of endearment designed to remind her of how precious she is to Him. He tells her that He is outside and wants to come in to her. He is so tender in his plea and he wants to be with her so desperately. Notice what he calls her…

1. My Sister - Speaking of the intimacy of their relationship. i.e., term "sister" was a term of affection that a husband might use for his wife. (The same kind of love that Jesus has for His bride - Ephesians 5:25.)

2. My Love - Speaking of the special place she holds in his heart. (How much Jesus loved us! - Romans 5:6-8)

3. My Dove - Speaks of the special peace that permeates their relationship. They are in a **joyous, glorious** relationship that has made them as one! (**We have been brought nigh to God through the blood of the Lord Jesus - Ephesians 2:12-13!**)

4. My Undefiled - **Speaks of the purity of their love.** There is nothing vulgar or evil transpiring here! No! There love is pure and she is pure! (**Justification - Romans 5:1**) (**The Call**)...

B. **The 'Complaint' Of The Bride**: (**Wife**) (**5:3**)
Her **response** is telling of her priorities. She tells him that she has already **washed her feet** and **is in the bed.** Simply put, she doesn't want to **get up and fool with him.**

How many of us have experienced something similar in our marriages? Something you would have **done without hesitation when you were first married now seems like pure labor, toil, or work.**

If we were honest, we would all have to **confess that we allow ourselves to become a little chilly in this department from time to time.**

Now, think about your walk with Jesus in that same context! Remember the early days of salvation?

- **When Church Services overflowing,**
- **When Bible Study was so exciting?**
- **When Prayer Time was a great adventure?**

Now, how many of us would have to admit that, **like the bride in our text,** we have **taken off our marching shoes** and that we have traded our **armor of the Spirit** for the **bedclothes of ease and leisure. Yes! We hav**e allowed ourselves to get **so comfortable** that just being with Jesus isn't as **exciting as it used to be**?

But there is good news, even when **church isn't so exciting** and Prayer Meeting and Bible Study just **do not thrill us anymore.**

I thank God that that does not have to be the **end of the story**—there **is a resurrection morning on the horizon! (The Complaint)**...

C. **The 'Compassion' Of The Bride**: **(5:4)**
When the **groom** (husband), tender words failed to arouse **the bride** (wife) interest toward him, He tries to open the door himself.

He fails to do this, but seeing he wanted to be with her so **badly stirs her heart** and she feels "*her heart begin to beat for him*". Let us not forget that **she too wants to be with him.**

How many of us will be willing to **come before him** this morning and **open the**

doors of our hearts to him afresh and anew today? How many will respond with love to the call of the Savior?

<u>"The Bride Dozing"</u>

<u>Exposition II</u>

II. <u>THE BRIDE DESIRING</u>: (6-8)

When she finally **rises from her bed and goes to the door,** she finds that **her beloved has already gone.** Then she remembers how she felt when she **did hear his voice.**

It was so intense that it caused her soul to faint within her. Now, he is gone. Still, she has been **reawakened to the need to be with him.**

A renewed desire is kindled within her **heart for her husband.** Now, just has he desired to be with her, she is filled with the desire to be with him

A. **The Direction Of Her Desire:** (5:6)

As she begins her search, notice what she says she is seeking. "*I sought HIM! I called HIM*".

- She makes no reference to **his wealth,** though he is the richest man in the land.

- She makes no reference to **his position,** though there is none more exalted than he.

- She makes no reference to **his power,** though there is none more powerful than he.

So it is with the child of God who **rediscovers how glorious Jesus is.** They aren't thrilled by **His power,** His **possessions** or by His **position.** They are thrilled just to be in **His presence.**

- ✓ When you and I reach a place where we are more 'interested' in **being with the Lord** than **getting something from the Lord;** that is a sure sign of spiritual growth.

- ✓ When we come to the place where **He fills our thoughts,** then we

have come to the place where He
holds first place.

You see, when we are in love with
the **Heavenly Bridegroom,** He will see to
it that **His Bride** is taken care of!
Instead of wanting **FROM Him,** let's get to
the place where we want **JUST Him.**

B. **The Depth Of Her Desire: (5:7, 8)**
As she went her way **looking for her
husband,** she was **humiliated** by the
watchmen. They took her 'veil' and they
'wounded' her.

But, she was not **deterred from her
mission!** Still **she sought him.** And, when
she could **not find him,** she **enlisted the
help of other women in the city.** She
tells them that she is *"Love sick."*

The whole point here is that she is
willing to **endure anything just to be
reunited with her husband.** She had been
indifferent to him before, now she **aches
to be in his arms.**

What a **lesson** for the church! What a **challenges** for the saints!

What **price we are willing to pay to be near our Lord**:

- o Are we will to **give up anything** that is necessary?
- o Are we willing to **suffer the humiliation** of the cross?
- o Are we willing to **bear His name?**

**When we reach the place where we are "*love sick*"!

**When we will pay the price to be close to Him!

**When we will be resolved to go all the way for the cause!

It is then that we are on our way to **higher heights** and deeper depth in the Lord. Question,,,,

1. What price are you **willing to pay** to become closer to the Lord Jesus?

2. Is your love for Jesus **all-consuming?** Does your love for everything else in life pale in comparison?

Do you love Him enough to **turn your back** on everyone else and everything else?

"The Bride Dozing"
"The Bride Desiring"
Exposition III

III. <u>THE BRIDE DESCRIBING</u>: (vv. 9-16)

In this passage the bride has had her **love rekindled** for the husband. Now, she wants nothing more than to be **reunited with him.**

Before, she was **too lazy to get out of bed to open the door for him,** now, **she tells us how she really fells about him!**

A. The Question Regarding Her Beloved: (5:9)

The daughters of Jerusalem ask this woman to tell them just what makes **this man more special than any other man.** She is challenged to tell them **why she loves him so much that she has become "*love sick*" over him.**

My Beloved, when we really fall in love with Jesus, there will always be those around you who will not understand you devotion to Him. They won't understand:

- Why you go to church three (3) times a week,
- Why you give a tenth and maybe more of your money,
- Why you talk about Him,
- What makes you tick!
    - **You will be called weird!
    - **You will be called different!

In fact, Peter tells us to give them an answer when they ask for a reason, *"But sanctify the Lord God in your hearts: and be ready always to give an answer to every man that asketh you a reason of the hope that is in you with meekness and fear" (1 Peter 3:15!)*

B. The Qualifications Of Her Beloved: (5:10-16a)
They want to know why she thinks he is **so special** and she tells them all

about him in verses 10-16. The language she uses **describes** him from head to toe and tells just how **lovely he is to her.** She tells them that he is the *"fairest among ten thousand."*

Then, she launches off on a **minute description** of his glories and his wonders. All of her terms are terms that describe **beauty, grace, strength** and **tenderness.** To her, he is the **perfect specimen of manhood.** To her, he is **absolutely perfect**!

When The Prophet Isaiah wrote about the coming Christ he said this, *"**For he shall grow up before him as a tender plant, and as a root out of a dry ground: he hath no form nor comeliness; and when we shall see him, there is no beauty that we should desire him.**",* (Isaiah 53:2).

Conclusion

So, in closing, my brothers and sisters, as we have described the loving and lovely relationship between the **bride and groom, this husband and wife**—we can be nothing but **thrilled,** as to how our relationship with the Lord, Jesus Christ **should mirror the same.**

If we had lived during the time of the Lord Jesus Christ and **seen Him on the street,** there would have been **nothing of beauty in Him that would have made us desire Him.**

But, how different He appears to the souls He has saved by His grace! Dearly beloved: **When we think of His…**

- ✓ **Love,** Jeremiah 31:3;
- ✓ **Grace,** Ephesians 2:8-9;
- ✓ **Death,** Revelations 1:5;
- ✓ **Blood,** 1 Peter 1:18-19;
- ✓ **Resurrection,** Revelations 1:18;
- ✓ **Call, St.** John 6:44;
- ✓ **Salvation,** Hebrews 7:25;
- ✓ **Keeping power,** 1 Peter 1:5;
- ✓ **Prepared Home, St.** John 14:1-3;
- ✓ **Return,** Revelations 22:20,

And, And not to mention His **"power"** and His **"glory",** how can *"We See Him"* as being less than **beautiful**? When we see God as He really is, that experience will **stir the heart to boundless praise** and **adoration**! He is the "*chiefest of ten billions!*" He is in a category all by Himself!)

We ought to offer up **'praise'** this morning for 'who' He is! If nothing else stirs us, let the **thought of Him** and **His beauty** cause us to **shout** the victory today!

C. The Quality Of Her Beloved:
(v. 16a)
Finally, she **exhausts** her vocabulary and sums Him up as being "*altogether lovely.*" She says, "*I have looked Him over from head to toe and I cannot find a single flaw in this man. He is absolutely perfect*!"

My friends, we can search the **farthest reaches** of the universe and you will **never find another like the Lord Jesus**! He is **altogether lovely**!

71

There is **no flaw** in Him! He is **full of glory** and **perfect in every way**! Those who **know Him love Him** and can see no flaw in the Lamb of God! Jesus Christ, because He is in a class by Himself!

In **6:1** - The **description** of the bride **awakens a desire** in the daughters of Jerusalem. So it is with this **'lost'** and **'dying'** world.

When the lost eyes are opened to the saving grace of Jesus Christ, it creates a **hunger within them for Him**.

In **6:4** through the end of the book there is an **unbroken communion** that is enjoyed by **these lovers**. Where does this message find your **heart this morning**?

Is it burning bright with a **boundless love** for the Lord Jesus? Or, have the cares of life and the attractions of this world caused your flame to become **an ember**? Are you hungry for Him?

➤ Do you remember a **better day in your walk with the Lord,** when you were **filled with love for Him**? Do you long for those days again? They are available!

All you need do is **seek Him with a heart** that is **stirred up in love for Him** and He will **fill you with His glory and presence.**

He wants to be with you more than you want to be with Him! Will you come to Him this morning? Now is the **time for decisions.** Now is the **time for commitment.** Come as the Lord may be leading you!

"A Heart For Him"
Joseph R. Rogers, Sr., D. Min.
Associate In Ministry

ATTENDING DRY BROOK UNIVERSITY

A Sermon By Dr. Joseph R. Rogers, Sr.
For The Martin Street Baptist Church
Raleigh, North Carolina 27601
Theme: Graduating With Honors
January 29, 2016

Scripture: "[2] And the word of the Lord came unto him, saying, [3] **Get thee hence, and turn thee eastward, and hide thyself by the brook Cherith, that is before Jordan.** [4] And it shall be, that thou shalt drink of the brook; and I have commanded the **ravens to feed thee there.** [5] So he (Elijah) went and did according unto the word of the Lord: for he (Elijah) went and dwelt by the **brook Cherith,** that is before Jordan. [6] And the "ravens" (bird) brought him **bread and flesh in the morning,** and **bread and flesh in the evening;** and **he 'drank' of the brook.** [7] And it came to pass after a while, that the **brook dried up,** because there had been **no rain in the land.**" **(1 Kings 17:2-7)**

Introduction

Boot camp for those who have served in the **military,** it is a place that is well remembered. It was a time of **brutal discipline, unending work, regimented training, cold fear** and **acute loneliness.**

Yet, it is in **boot camp** where young undisciplined and sometimes out of control boys and girls are developed into "**mature" disciplined** strong soldiers.

A soldier would never be able to serve on the battlefield unless he/she has first been trained and equipped for battle.

In boot camp, prospective soldiers have their self-will striped away and they lose any **rebellion** that may in their heart.

They learn to follow order from a superior without question and they learn to follow their leader, even to death, if necessary.

Of course, the positive side of all the **training,** the **discipline** and the pressure is that the **soldier grows stronger, more disciplined** and **more mature**. You might say that boot camp is much like enrolling in disciplined **university program**.

Well beloved, we might say as believers that God has placed each of us in He has a **Dry Brook University,** to **train us,** to **impart knowledge** that we might **gain the wisdom** required to 'walk' and 'live' **VICTORIOUS IN HIM.**

The Prophet Elijah we enroll in Dry Brook University in the verses of our focus today. As with this Prophet before we can be trusted to **stand on Carmel,** we must first **graduate from Dry Brook University.**

It is a well-known **institution of higher learning,** it is **fully accredited** by the Father, Son and Holy Spirit **accreditation board** and it offers degrees in a **variety of disciplines.**

Before God can place us on the **battlefield** as a soldier of the cross, He must first send us to and get us through **boot camp.** This isn't a truth we **enjoy thinking about,** but it stands to reason that before God can **really use us,** He must first 'remove' from us **that which hinders His will from going forth in our lives—OURSELVES!**

Therefore, let's join Elijah this morning as he enrolls at **Dry Brook University.** His experience contains **several elements of truth** that we need to **ingest, digest and process in our lives. First…**

This message for today is divided in four (4) parts, of which, one setting would over **feed us** and be **too lengthy;** therefore I will share it as led by **The Holy Spirit;** as its benefits to our **spiritual edification in this manner.**

Part #1-The Place God Ordain, Part #2-The Promises God Offers, Part #3-The Plan God Orders, and part #4-The Problem God Orchestrates.

I. <u>THE PLACE GOD ORDAIN</u>:

(v. 2-4)

The Prophet Elijah has just stood before the King of Israel and delivered the **'message of judgment'** that God had given him. Now, the next word from God is command to **'hide'** himself away.

You see, God has a way of **always getting us into things** that we did not ask for. Well the good news is, God always has a **plan** and He is always **in control** of the situation. In The Prophet case, God wants to **transform** Elijah from *Elijah the Tishbite* (**17:1**) into *Elijah the Man of God* (**17:24**). To accomplish this, God sends Elijah to school.

A. <u>The Name Of That Place</u>:
(2-3) (*Cherith*)

The word means "*to cut off, to cut down*". God has cut off Elijah from public view so that He might **cut him down to size**. The biggest problem in each of our lives is not "The Devil", it is OUR **"EGO"**, or might I say, **"SUPEREGO"**—the desire to be in charged!

One of the *hardest lessons* the child of God will ever learn is that God **must send** us to 'Cherith' before He can **use us for His glory.** God has to **hide us** away and **cut us down,** bring us under spiritual discipline, so that "His Image", "His Plan", and "Our Position" in Him might be may be **clear to us.**

Like as when the 'Silversmith' heats the silver and skims off the 'dross' (trash, scum or waste), so that he can see his 'image in the silver'. Without question, we are so **full ourselves** such that, God must apply heat (situations challenges) to us, in order that He might to bring us to that place where we see **less of self** and more of **His image.** (Ezekiel 22:20-22)
 <u>"The Name Of That Place: (Cherith)"</u>

B. **The Nature Of That Place:**
(v. 3)
It is a hidden place designed especially for those who are children of God who loves God. Note the command from God, *"Hide thyself"*. "Cherith" is by nature a 'hard' and 'lonely' place. Here

Elijah would be **removed from the spotlight** and **dwell alone** while the Lord worked out His will in his life.

Of all the lessons that we can learn from these verses, one of the most powerful is that we must **never overlook the power of the hidden life**. It is a place, hidden away from public view that **Elijah, as well as you and I became a man/woman of God.**

It is here that Elijah learns to 'trust**' God totally.

It is here that Elijah learns to 'lean**' on the Lord.

- ✓ You see, before we can ever **give out**, we must first **take in.**

- ✓ You see, before we can pour anything out of our vessels, we must first allow God to put something in them.

My friends, never forget that God knows where we are and He will never leave us by ourselves—He will never send us anywhere without **equipping** and **preparing** us for the **task or journey.**

- If He has sent us to 'Cherith', He is there with us.
- If He gives us a task, He will give us the **power, knowledge** and **warewithal** to come out **VICTORIOUS.**
  "The Nature Of The Place: (Hide Thyself)"

C. <u>The Necessity Of That Place</u>: (v.4)

Notice the use of the word *"there"*. There suggest, **here, nearby, around--** Cherith was a **specific place.** It was the **only place** Elijah **could be and be right with God.** If he had gone anywhere else, he would have **starved to death.**

God had **specifically ordered provisions for Elijah** and He had ordered them to be **delivered** to "Cherith"--the only place destined for The Prophet Elijah to be by God. As with Jonah, when the Lord **sends us** to a place in life, there is the tendency to want to be **somewhere else.**

Rather than going to **"Nineveh"**-the planned place, we are onward bound to **"Joppa"**—the unplanned place—totally in the opposition direction. Someone is **saying** and I hear you loudly---After all…

- Who likes pain?
- Who likes sickness?
- Who likes financial trouble?
- Who likes to struggle?
- Who likes disappointment?

What we must learn, my brothers and sister, is that if God **sends us to a Cherith,** He knows what He is doing. If we find ourselves in a **difficult situation,** we must trust God and submit to His will for our lives and learn that God has our back.

Again, we have only two choices. The first is **"rebellion".** We can fight God and **'stay'** in our **'Cherith'** longer than planned by God, or **"follow"** God plan as

did The Prophet Elijah and submit to God
that He might work out His plan for/in
our lives.

In other words, you can either
choose to be **miserable** as you go through
the difficulties of life alone or you can
choose to **rejoice** in the will of the
Lord.
You see, while in **"Cherith"**:
- It may be a **hard place.**
- It may be a **place that hurts.**
- It may be a **frightening place.**

But, I have learned over this almost
forty (40) years, that it does not matter
the **degree** of the **challenge** of situation:

- ✓ If God is with us.
- ✓ If God is watching over us,
- ✓ If God as ordained us to be
  there—there is no victory for the
  enemy.

As children of the Most High God:

- We will enjoy a **'dance'** of victory,
- We will enjoy a **'shout'** of victory,
- We will enjoy a **'praise'** of victory, because...

I know that if the Lord **ordained** a place or position for us, our **best and only option** is to just says, Yes! Lord—from the bottom of my heart to the depths of my soul—Yes! Lord.

"I. The Place God Ordained"

II. <u>THE PROMISE GOD OFFERES</u>: (4-6)

The Prophet Elijah is sent to the middle of **nowhere to hide.** Of course, we know that God sent him there for two primary reasons: *"Protection" and "Training".*

God promise **The Prophet Elijah** that his needs would be met while he is experiencing, **"Cherith".** The lesson of these verses is this: *God's call is always accompanied by God's provisions.*

He will never send you to a place in life that He does not give us *"ALL"* that we need to **pass the course**. The appointed place of God is always complete with His **provisions** for that place!) **The Promise of God...**

A. <u>Involved Advance Planning</u> (4)
Notice that before the need arose, God already had the provisions in place. God made sure to form that a little brook was available just for Elijah. Before The Prophet go to 'Cherith', God had already commanded the **ravens** to supply a nice meal.

What does this assures us? Well, this lets us know that nothing catches God by **surprise**. When challenges come into our lives, God, unlike us do not say, *"Oh no! What am I going to do? How will I keep this man alive?"*

Regardless of the **circumstance** or **difficulty**, God has already prepared the path that we will take:

Psalm 37:23-"²³ The steps of a good man are ordered by the Lord: and he delighteth in his way".

2 Corinthians 12:9-"⁹ And he said unto me, My grace is sufficient for thee: for my strength is made perfect in weakness. Most gladly therefore will I rather glory in my infirmities, that the power of Christ may rest upon me".

B. **Involved Amazing Provision** (v.6)
God used a **bubbling brook** and **ravens** to feed Elijah while he was stationed at **"Cherith"**. This is remarkable because ravens are scavengers. They feed of the flesh of the dead. Yet, God used them to bring life sustaining food to The Prophet.

Have you ever wondered where they got the food? Maybe from Ahab and Jezebel's table his enemies) At any rate, God **suspended** the **"laws of nature"** to meet the **need of His child.**

Never forget that God knows what you need. If He has too, He will move 'heaven' and 'earth' to see that our needs are met. He knows where we are and He knows where the **provisions for us are.** He will direct **our path** to the place where He can meet your need.

Philippians 4:19-"[19]But my God shall supply all your need according to his riches in glory by Christ Jesus".

C. Involved Abundant Peace (v. 5)
Note the phrase, *"So he went and did according to the word of the Lord."* When God called, Elijah simply stepped out in faith and obeyed. That is one of the secrets to surviving **your "Cherith Experiences"**!

Faith and trust in God, brings us to a place where we do not **question God,** that is, when He speaks, **we respond** by doing what we are told to do. You see, when we are on **God's payroll,** He will pay our way. However, when you **choose to walk a path He has not ordained,** we will pay our own way.
Again, as mentioned previously, about the Prophet Jonah in **Jonah 1:1-3.**

God's servants must come to the place where they trust God **absolutely.** Elijah had nothing but the **promise of God,** yet for him that was **sufficient** to let him know that all would be well.

    "I. The Place God Ordained"
    "II. The Promise God Offered"

III. THE PLAN GOD ORDERES: (5-6)
A. It Was A Sovereign Plan

Notice that God was in absolute control of the situation. The **ravens** did as He had commanded them and they brought bread and flesh to the prophet twice per day. The **brook** continued to provide liquid refreshment as well.

All of this was ordered by the Lord to teach the prophet that God was in **absolute control** of what happened. When the Lord puts you in a place where you can do nothing but trust Him, He had done you the **greatest favor** that He can extend, outside of salvation. When we come to the place where we are **trusting Him and Him alone,** we have reached a great level of growth.

B. It Was A Satisfying Plan

It is **satisfying** because Elijah enjoyed the fulfillment of the Lord's promises to him. He received just what he Lord told him he would.

Nothing means as much to a **suffering saint** as the peace of knowing that **God is in control**! We may **not like the situation** in which we find ourselves, but if we know that God is going to take care of us, then we can be satisfied anywhere, with anything.

C. It Was A Submissive Plan

Notice that **verse 5** tells us that *"he went and dwelt by the brook."* The word *"dwelt"* means *"to live"*.

Elijah wasn't headed out there for an overnight camping trip. He intended to live in that place until the Lord came and told him to **go somewhere else**. Have you submitted to **your Cherith**?

The whole purpose in **God's plan** was to help Elijah come to the place where he could trust God for one day at a time. I would imagine that there was some **question in the prophet's heart that first evening.**

Would there be flesh and bread in the morning? But, as the days passed and God proved Himself to be **faithful and trustworthy,** Elijah learned to **walk by faith.** Friends, that is where the Lord wants to bring us as well!

The Bible tells us that *"the just shall live by faith.",* **Romans 1:17.** God wants us to be **totally dependent upon Him.** He wants us to rest in **His arms by faith, without fear.** He will cut us off and cut us down to teach us to trust Him fully!)

"I. The Place God Ordained"
"II. The Promise God Offered"
"III. The Plan God Ordered"

IV. <u>THE PROBLEM GOD ORCHESTRATED</u> (v. 7)

A. <u>A Dry Brook</u>

This steam of life giving water ran dry! Imagine how Elijah must have felt as he watched that **stream grow smaller each day**. As the days passed, the **little brook began to get narrow**. Then, one day it was all gone! Nothing was left but a dry stream bed.

This happens to us as well! And what we must do is not panic and **lose of temperament**. As in all experiences we must hold fast to the God who **save us**, **call us** and **provides for us**. In these experiences...

- ✓ That job that we have invested our lives in dries up.
- ✓ That mate that we have given walks out on us.
- ✓ Our health seems to be breaking down.

Conclusion

So, In closing, my brothers and sisters, I am glad that I attended, **"Dry Brook University"**. Every day has not Sunday and the Sun does not shine every day. But one thing I can tell you is every step of the way, **"God was right there"**.

Well, again, regardless who we are; our **class, status or position,** the brooks of our lives will **dry up**! Good News, we are faced with these kinds of trials, we must **never lose sight of two great truths and they are…**

1. *The God Who provides the water can also withhold the water.*
2. *A dry brook is not always a sign of God's displeasure.*

- It happened to **"Abraham"** when he was called on to offer up Isaac.
- It happened to **"Joseph"** as he ministered in Potiphar's house.

- It happened to **"Paul"** as he faithfully served God in Lystra.

- It happened to **"Jesus"** as He agonized in Gethsemane and as He gave His life a ransom for sin on Calvary.

Sometimes, God allows our brook to dry up because God is **pleased with us** and **desires to take us on to new and better things**

Sometimes, God allows the brook to dry up because we **are guilty of trusting the brook more than we trust Him.**

We are to learn to look to **The Lord,** the giver of the gift and not to gifts! Even when the "gifts" are gone, the giver is still available to do the impossible.

I can hardly imagine how Elijah must have felt as that brook dried up before his eyes. Did he feel abandoned and forsaken? Did he feel that God has somehow let him down?

For some reason, God will often allow His people to sit by a **drying brook.** When it happens, and it will, never believe for an instant that God has **forgotten about you or forsaken you.**

If you are **in His will,** then you can **rest in His promise to take care of you.**

We need to come to an understanding that God **dries up the brooks of life because He has something even bigger just down the road.**

Sometimes the brooks dry up because you have done everything correctly as designed by God. Remember when God sends us to "Dry Brook University it is purposed and Plan:

- ✓ He is **training us!**
- ✓ He is **maturing us!**
- ✓ He us **equipping us!**
- ✓ He is **building** us!

We become an alumnus of *"Dry Brook University"*, we're place in a position and a posture—to look Satan square in the eyes and let him know that there will not be any trouble, unless he starts some.

As **children of The Most High God,** may we come to the place where we realize that everything that happens in your life God is able to remix it to our good **(All Things), (We're More Than Conquerors-- Roman 8:28).**

- If there is a **physical need**---give it to the Lord!
- If there is a **spiritual need**–give it to the Lord!
- If you are **standing watching looking your brook dry up**–give it to the Lord!

Whatever! Whatever! Whatever the need, Jesus can meet it today---just give it to Him! Graduate from, **"Dry Brook University"**.

"Dry Brook University".

Joseph R. Rogers, Sr., D. Min.
Associate In Ministry

"IF"

A Sermon By Dr. Joseph R. Rogers, Sr.
For The Believers Church Of Deliverance
Raleigh, North Carolina 27610
Theme: Possibility, In Spite
September 1, 2012

Scripture: "If my people which are **called** by My name, shall "**humble**" themselves, and "**pray**", and "**seek my face**", and "**turn from their wicked ways**", "**then**" (after that, subsequently, followed by) will I - **hear**- from heaven, and will -**forgive**- their sin, and will -**heal**- their land." **(II Chronicles 7:14)**

Introduction

I am delighted to be with you today to share in Word Of The Lord. It is by the **grace of God** that we are among the living, that is, above the ground and not beneath. We're breathing today not because of our **good deeds or righteous living**, but only by the **grace, love** and **mercy** of The Divine, God Almighty.

This is why we must never **take God for granted**; that is, to say He **owes us**

96

all that He allows us to **have** and **enjoy in life. The Prophet Isaiah** makes it clear and plain, *"But we are -all- as an unclean thing, and -all- our righteousnesses are as filthy rags; and we -all- do fade as a leaf; and our iniquities, like the wind, have taken us away"* (64:6).

So, today as we go through in this life it would best for us to do the best of our ability **'edifying'** one another, rather than **'condemning'** each other. Why? Because **'if'** God gave us **our just reward;** it would certainly not be **'death'** and not **'eternal life'** based on **your merits.**

This text for today is **very** "interesting" and "timely" for the **development and maturity of our spirit man.** When we fail to follow God's principles and follow through with His **destined plan;** it is **an indictment** on the **awesomeness** of His divine **character, integrity** and **intelligence.**

The message today is **foundation** on a simple **English word** that is in itself, is very weighty, call, "__IF__". A Word that we use all of the time without thinking about **its affect** upon what we are **announcing** or **professing**.

This small two letter word, __"IF"__ is used on to continue many of our phrases, quotes, or sentences. For example, "I **will make it, __-if-__ else does not come up**" or __"-If-__ **I obey God's Principles, I will receive His many blessings**".

If can be used as a "conjunction" used to **indicate a modification** of the left sided phrase.

If can be used a "conjunction" **us to connect words, phrases, clauses, or sentences.**

- **If my people**...would do as I ask them to do...**then I will do something that is both rewarding and refreshing.**

- **If my people**...would do as I ask them to do...**then I would cause** their enemies to be at peace with them.

- **If my people**...would do as I ask them to do...**weep make endure for the night but joy cometh in the morning.**

From this, we must concluded that one of the biggest words in the **human language** is the little two letter word, "If".

Exposition I

So, our text for today is **mighty in power;** such that it has the ability to change the course of our situations, if, "**If**", is used or applied properly.

- If is more **powerful** than an **atomic bomb**!
- If is more **deadly** than a **hydrogen bomb**!
- It is more **explosive** than TNT!

The Word of God is saturated with some big **'ifs'** that **has/will make** a big difference in the lives of humanity and **change** the course of nature. According to my calculating there are some **1522** of them in the Scriptures: To Name a Few...

- ✓ I John 1:9--"<u>If</u> we confess our sins he is faithful and just to forgive us our sins and to cleanse us from all unrighteousness. If we walk in the light as He is in the light we have fellowship one with the other."

- ✓ **St Matthew 9:21**--"<u>If</u> I may but touch the hem of His garment I shall be made whole. If I be lifted up I will draw all men unto me.

- ✓ **Colossians 3:1**--"<u>If</u> ye be risen with Christ, speak those things which are above."

- ✓ I John 1:8--"<u>If</u> we say that we have no sin, we deceive ourselves, and the truth is not in us."

But, the biggest <u>'if'</u> in the whole Bible is to be found in the text, **2 Chronicles 7:14.**

God says, "**If ye will----then I will.**"

- o **"Revival"** will come, if people humble themselves and pray.
- o **"Forgiveness"** comes, if people humble themselves and pray.
- o **"Healing"** comes, if people humble themselves and pray.

Speaking to His chosen vessels God says,

Exposition II
II. **If my people which are called by my name...etc.**

God's people are called by His name. Here, **God's reputation** is involved. David in **Psalms 23:3** said "He leadeth me in the paths of righteousness on account of His own reputation."

Peculiar people have obligations to fulfill. Jesus said, **"Ye are the salt of the earth." If you lose your saltiness you lose your worthiness**. We are God's representatives, the people which are called by His name.

Jesus said, "**Ye are the light of the world. Let your light so shine that God may be glorified by your light.**" If your light has gone out how great is your darkness! God's representatives, people called by His name. Next...

Exposition II
I. ...humble themselves...etc.

Humility in those strenuous times seems to be a grace gone out of style. Yet humility is the **gateway to God.** The first blessed in the Sermon on the Mount is for **the humble. "Blessed are the poor in spirit for theirs is the kingdom of heaven."**

A humbling which comes when we look within, when we place our lives alongside of Christ's life, when like John the Baptist we say, **"I am not worthy to unlace His shoes."**

This is a humility like the **prodigal son** demonstrated when he came home to the

Father's house in rags and poverty and said, "I have sinned against heaven and earth and am no more worthy to be called thy son." **Humility** is the **turning of the whole heart,** the whole soul to God. Next…

II. <u>And pray, and seek my face and turn from wicked ways…etc</u>.

Prayer is communicating to God in a reverent way. Prayer is talking to God with a **sincere heart, mind and soul.** The best time to pray to God is during times of **'peace'** and **'plenty'.**

- ✓ **The Centurion** prayed and his servant was healed!
- ✓ **The Lady with blood issue** prayed and God touched her with His anointing.
- ✓ **The blind man** prayed and God gave him his sight and he saw men as trees.
- ✓ **David** prayed and God forgave him for is sins and transgressions.

When we pray with our whole heart, mind and spirit; something good is going to happen. It does not matter if we are poor, crushed, broken or of sorry heart we can go **directly to God in prayer.**

There is something else that we must to in our praying and that is... Next

Iva. <u>**And turn from their wicked**</u>
<u>**ways**</u>.
God can do nothing for **the proud.** We must turn from our **pride of positions, pride of economics,** and **pride of culture.** God hates the **pride of self-sufficiency** and **false values.** We must depend upon Jesus Christ, **glorying in Him and not ourselves.**

Conclusion
So, in closing it is a wonderful thing to know that "If" we do the Lord will, He will **assure us** that everything will be alright. **"If we do---The God will then..."** Next...

III. <u>**Then I will hear from heaven,**</u>
<u>**and forgive their sins**</u>

- When we humbled ourselves!
- When we have prayed!

104

- When we have sought The Lord's face,
- When we have met God's conditions---then we will hear from heaven and the Lord will **forgive** our sins and He will **heal** the land.

✓ Our land may be **our own 'souls'**. God will forgive us **if** we humble ourselves.

✓ Our land may be **our 'homes'**. God will heal the breach between families **if** we will humble ourselves.

✓ Our land may be **our 'churches Conditions'**, God will make better the relationship between the church membership, if we will humble ourselves.

What will you do with the **if's in the Bible**? **What if God…**.

- What if, **GOD** did not take the time to bless us today because we couldn't take the time to thank Him yesterday?

- What if, **GOD** decided to stop leading us tomorrow because we didn't follow Him today?

- What if, we never saw another flower bloom because we grumbled when **GOD** sent the Rain?

- What if, **GOD** didn't walk with us today because we failed to recognize it as His day?

- What if, **GOD** took away the Bible tomorrow because we would not read it today?

- What if, **GOD** took away His message because we failed to listen to the messenger?

- What if, **GOD** didn't send His only begotten son because He wanted us to pay the price for sin.

- What if, the door of the church was closed because we did not open the door of our heart?

- What if, GOD stopped loving and caring for us because we failed to love and care for others?

- What if, GOD would not hear us today because we would not listen to Him?

- What if, GOD answered our prayers the way we answer His call to service?

- What if, GOD met our needs the way we give Him our lives?

Yes! Again, "If my people which are called by my name will humble themselves and pray and seek my face and turn from their evil ways, -then- I will hear from heaven, and forgive their sin, and heal their lands."

"IF"

Joseph R. Rogers, Sr., D. Min.
Associate In Ministry

II. The Author's Contacts Informatin And Other works

A. Mailing Address:

1313 Ujamaa Drive, Raleigh, NC 27610

Phone No. (919) 208-0200

B. Email Address:

jroger3420@aol.com

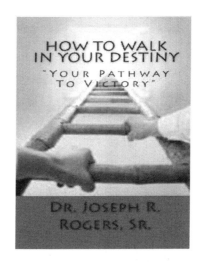

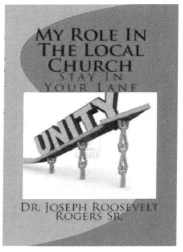

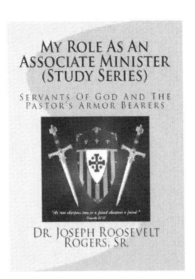

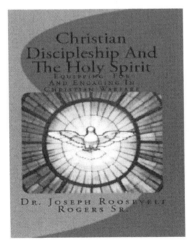

111

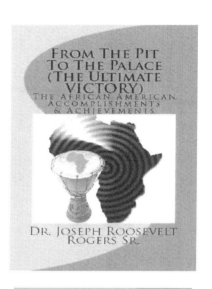

FROM THE PIT
TO THE PALACE
(THE ULTIMATE
VICTORY)
THE AFRICAN AMERICAN
ACCOMPLISHMENTS
& ACHIEVEMENTS

DR. JOSEPH ROOSEVELT
ROGERS SR.

MARRIAGE
GOD'S WAY
"KEEP THE FIRE
BURNING"

DR. JOSEPH R. ROGERS, SR.

SERMON SERIES 39S (FOR ALL OCCASIONS)

SERMON OUTLINES FOR EASY PREACHING

DR. JOSEPH ROOSEVELT ROGERS, SR.

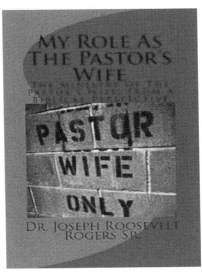

MY ROLE AS THE PASTOR'S WIFE

DR. JOSEPH ROOSEVELT ROGERS, SR.

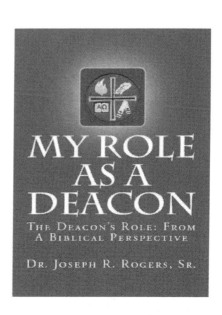

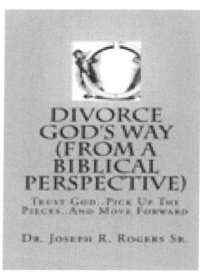

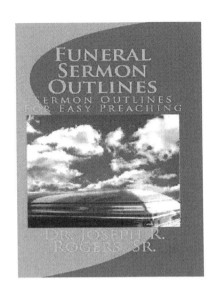

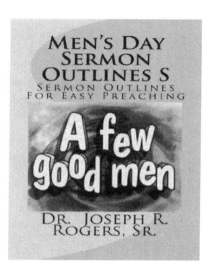

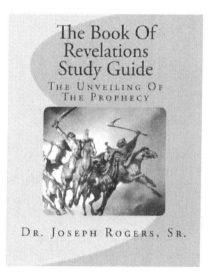

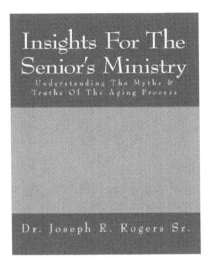

Insights For The
Senior's Ministry
Understanding The Myths &
Truths Of The Aging Process

Dr. Joseph R. Rogers Sr.

BLESSED AND HIGHLY
FAVORED A STUDY
SERIES: PHYSICAL &
SPIRITUAL BLESSINGS
Dr. Joseph Rogers, Sr.

"WHOSO FINDETH A WIFE FINDETH A GOOD THING AND OBTAINETH FAVOR OF THE LORD". (PROVERBS 18:22)

INSIGHTS FOR CHOOSING A COMPANION
Securing The Right Companion
Dr. Joseph Rosevelt Rogers Sr.

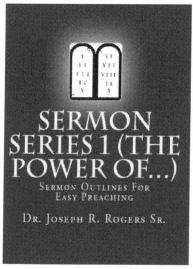

SERMON SERIES 1 (THE POWER OF...)
Sermon Outlines For Easy Preaching

Dr. Joseph R. Rogers Sr.

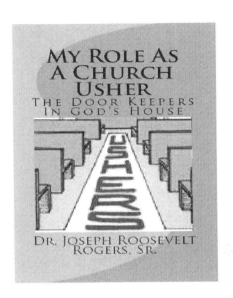

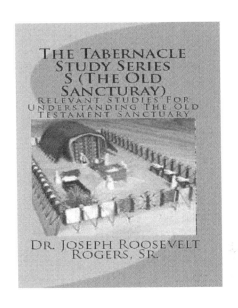

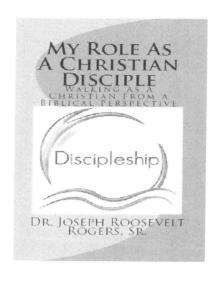

III. Notes

Notes Con't.

52959572R00071

Made in the USA
Charleston, SC
29 February 2016